# Calm is the New Happy

# Calm Is The New Happy

## How To Get There In Five Minutes

BY

DEBBIE D'AQUINO

Cover image from depositphotos.com
Cover design by Angie at pro_ebookcovers
Book design by Diane D'Aquino Landskroener

*Focus on the peace that is around you at all times.*

www.calmisthenewhappy.com

*"There is nothing either good or bad,*
*but thinking makes it so."*
~ William Shakespeare

*"Life is like playing a violin solo in public and*
*learning the instrument as one goes on."*
~ Samuel Butler

*"The greatest evils are from within us; and from*
*ourselves also we must look for the greatest good."*
~ Jeremy Taylor

*"Whether you think you can or think you can't,*
*you are right."*
~ Henry Ford

*"Without a new direction, our minds will continue to*
*create exactly what we've always created."*
~ Mary Morrissey

*"I don't know the key to success, but the key to failure*
*is to try to please everyone."*
~ Bill Cosby

*"If the only prayer you ever said was Thank You,*
*it would be enough."*
~ Meister Eckhart

# CONTENTS

# Finding My Calm Within

When I started working on this book, I shared the title with a number of friends. I was checking reactions to know if the title was a good one and to see if it would evoke any type of interest. Without probing or asking what they thought, I received one of two comments. It was either, "That's a good title," or "I gotta read that book!"

I liked hearing those words, "I gotta read that book!" It reinforced my desire to write a simple solution to a growing need in many of us. Clearly I get it; it's not so much we are searching for calm as much as it is about releasing our stress.

Stress and overwhelm have crept into our lives as accepted emotions. Everyone struggles with them now and again. There is a perverse misconception that we are not valuable in today's busy world if we're not stressed. We're not working hard enough or taking on enough if we're not overwhelmed. This kind of thinking is driving mini-panic attacks and sleepless nights. We face far more chores than we have hours in the day. We're striving for the best in everything and see little time to accomplish the goal. As crazy as it sounds, we are creating this entire flurry in our minds.

I'm reminded of a great comment I heard during an online interview with Jeffrey Gignac. Gignac is a world leader in brainwave entrainment. He said, "What's interesting about human beings is that we are the only mammal on the planet that can actually be sitting comfortably in a heated house, in perfect comfort with food and water and get all stressed out about things that have never happened. Bears don't do that. (chuckle) No mammal does that. But human beings are able to do that. And we do it often. And we do it out of habit."

Do we do it on purpose? Invite stressful thinking into our lives? I don't think so. What is this overwhelming stress that seems to arrive uninvited? How does it get created? Why is it so hard to release? Can it truly affect my mood, attitude, and immune system like recent magazine articles suggest? I used to be so calm, easy-going, and happy; what the heck happened?

Even the most stressed person can become calm in a very short amount of time. It's easier than you think. If that doesn't seem possible, you will be interested in the recent scientific research I've uncovered. It proves, through peer-reviewed studies, that a simple set of techniques can reduce stress to minimal levels within minutes. Anyone open to learning can apply these easy techniques. Even the most stressful life can become calm, all you need is the desire to make it happen.

Learning to switch your stress into calmness quickly takes a little practice, especially if you want to "get there in 5 minutes." *Anything* new requires an understanding of its process to achieve it.

You perform daily routines without a thought, but at one time those routines required learning. Easy five minute jobs took much longer to accomplish on the first attempt.

Here's young Jack shaving for the first time. There isn't much to tackle but he's excited nonetheless. He lathers up with foaming cream. The cream itself feels rather light and frothy and he's not sure if it is too much or too little. He enjoys the scent and wonders if it will tingle or burn when it is applied to his skin. With slight hesitation, on it goes, too thick in one area and too thin in another. He gets absorbed in perfecting its evenness. He sees his image in the mirror for the first time with a white beard. He admires how handsomely his eyes stand out when his face is covered in cream. He checks his new razor for cleanliness and sharpness. Lots of little distractions cause the entire five minute process to take much longer this first go around. Once Jack is familiar with all the particulars of shaving and he is comfortable with the process, it's quick and easy to get the job done. It is only after many days of practice, repeating the same easy steps, he becomes proficient at shaving. Now he is a master; he can do it in five minutes!

Let's look at 14-year-old Jeannette. She is applying makeup for the first time. It's exciting, time-consuming and a bit frustrating. Fifteen minutes flies by just figuring out the color choices and selection of brushes. Another thirty minutes pass while applying layers of foundation, shadowing and highlights. She attempts lining her eyes and adds mascara to the lashes. A glob falls to her cheek as she delicately swabs it away with a q-tip and reapplies the missing blush. She studies her face closely for what to do next. With a shaky hand she outlines her lips with liner and finishes her pout with a bright touch of lip color. For a first try, Jeanette is pleased with her facial artwork but wonders how do they do this everyday? I'll have to get up an extra hour earlier!

It is persistent practice through multiple trials that brings swiftness to the job. Repeat the same procedures. Let go of distractions. Stay focused on the goal. It's the repetition that perfects the skill; repeat the procedure with confidence and determination. Once one becomes comfortable with the applications and understands the process, it's quick and easy to get the job done. After many days of practice, you grow proficient, and you master the process. It becomes a cinch! You can do it in 5 minutes!

A similar process applies when releasing stress and replacing with calm; it may take you a few tries. Repeating the steps and staying persistent with your practice will get you there quickly. I will also share with you a few simple tools I use to achieve calmness almost immediately. All of these tools you already have at hand. We will just apply a different perspective and PRESTO! Calmness is yours. Stress be gone!

Let me ask, do you ever have a pit in your stomach because you can't make a decision?

Do you ever get frozen by indecision because too many options confuses which is best for you?

Do you ever have your mind going in circles because there's just too much to do, too many things to sort out?

Do you ever have tightness in your neck and back because you don't have the money to pay the bills? Do you have a lost, sick feeling wondering "Where is the money going to come from?"

Do you ever feel like you're drowning? You're working so hard, you're doing everything you can to stay on top, yet you're drowning in life?

My answer was "Yes" to all those questions as I moved through my daily life. I was drowning! Along with sorting, aching, wondering, forgetting, and feeling insecure, my life was whirling nowhere and I had forgotten how to dream my way out of it.

Have you heard this granny story? "While on vacation with my son and his family, I shared a room with my 4-year-old granddaughter. One morning when she awoke, she started retelling all the nice dreams she had through the night. I told her how I wished I was able to dream like that. The 4-year-old quipped, 'But Granny, you can't because you snore too much.'"

Cute! And point well made. We don't quiet our minds long enough to dream anymore. Even while sleeping we are making noise. The chatter doesn't stop. It's time to bring dreaming back. Dreaming that includes an inspiring life. Dream up a life to be shared with others and make a difference. Dream up a life that can face any challenges with confidence and clarity.

As you walk with me through this book, I have high hopes you are about to jump from gloom to bloom. You will find a new trust and a new excitement in your dream life that is right under your nose.

## Stress Attacks Then Pain Reacts

As I continually strive to create my dream life, I still get attacked by stress. Even though I have studied many varied forms of meditation (from the far reaches of seeking perfect enlightenment to the less stringent mindfulness for the western world) I still get attacked by stress. Life is a bumpy road and knowing tricks to navigate its challenges makes the ride a lot smoother.

Looking back, I can see a lot of irony in my life. There were so many situations that were highly stressful for me and while I had learned meditation and calming strategies for those situations, I would forget to apply them. Like a knee-jerk reaction, when I'm most stressed I can't think straight. By habit I would turn to my upbringing, I would pray. Prayer gave me hope things would get better. Both prayer and meditation serve to connect us to our higher source. I pray and meditate every day. They work very well together but they are two different things.

In Prayer, we use our brain and thoughts to converse with God. We are in conversation.

In Meditation, we relax our brain and thoughts and use our feeling center to be connected with God. We are in reception.

I was in my early twenties when I left the east coast with a friend and ventured to California. California opened new avenues of thought, lifestyle, and appreciation of nature. I found myself drawn to a spiritual calling. Although I had studied business administration in college, being tied to a desk job was far from my heart's desire. Exploring my inner being was a new high for me. I loved yoga and meditation. I wanted to do it every day, all day. I completed a teacher's course for the Indra Devi Method of Yoga Asanas and Meditation at the Kamala Ma Yoga School in San Juan Capistrano, California.

Earning my certification as a yoga instructor gave me wings to share my new passion. Soon I was teaching in YMCAs and adult education programs. I loved guiding the inner bliss of yoga-meditation and seeing body strength improve in my students. This beautiful method of discovering the self was new and exciting, like the honeymoon state of a blossoming love.

I was dedicated to this mission over the next three years. I enjoyed teaching hundreds of students the ways of a yogi. At the same time, I had another artistic passion burning to express itself. I had been designing and sewing my own clothing since I was 8 years old. I wanted to turn my favorite hobby into a profession as well. I found the courage to apply my AA degree from Hagerstown Community College to enroll in an accelerated program at the Fashion Institute of Design and Merchandising, Los Angeles. I was awarded a Design Certification in Fashion. Within a week of graduation, I was hired as head designer for a lingerie manufacturer and my new career was launched. For the next twenty years I excelled as a fashion designer for multiple corporations throughout Los Angeles.

Fashion designing can be glamorous and exciting. For me it was the right medium to inspire artistic expression, vision, and challenge. As part of my job, I traveled cities in Italy, France, England, and the U.S. to research the latest fashions. I loved the travel involved. Everywhere I looked my designer's eye saw trends and color palettes, shapes, silhouettes, and innovating fabrications. I mixed the old with the new. I was filled with inspiration and enthusiasm. I thrived on sketching a never-ending supply of ideas that poured through me. My position included fun responsibilities like dressing models for catalog shoots and runway shows and receiving accolades for saleable creations. Those were the many highlights of my job. It was the juice that would push me forward to keep giving more and more of myself.

Behind the scenes, glamour took a back seat. Grueling deadlines and pressures showed no mercy. Expectations from major buyers never let up. It's understandable, too, because buyers are pressured to keep their store on the cutting edge with products that are better than the last. It is the designer's responsibility to create desirable products that produce sales for the entire company. My ideas were securing the payroll for hundreds of fellow workers and for the companies buying our product. I felt the continual pressures of the job breaking down my body's endurance. As the years passed, crippling neck pain and backaches crept into my body from leaning over drafting tables and etching out pattern work. I was slowed down with carpel tunnel burning in my wrists but it did not stop me from sketching the next collection. Migraine headaches became a monthly event. Weekly exercise became a challenge. Love relationships swept me off my feet, took me to highs, dropped me to lows, and left me broken hearted. My heart ached from broken dreams while my body ached from painful stress.

I handled the mounting pressures and stress fairly well for the first twelve years of my career. Then I started feeling numbness on the front thigh of each leg. The numbing left my skin cold and lifeless. I had no choice but to continue working and put up with the numbness. As the weeks passed the numbness in my legs was accompanied with lower back pain. The reason for the numbness had made itself obvious, an inflamed sciatic nerve. At night I battled pain to find a comfortable sleeping position. My hips and thighs ached. I didn't submit to over-the-counter pain remedies often but on occasion I had to take them to find relief. I was told by the chiropractor to stay away from the pain relievers, so most nights I would grimace through the pain. Then back to work the next day.

About two years into this, my pain-body started multiplying. My center spine bulged with herniated discs. If you've ever experienced this type of pain, you know how badly this can hurt. Everything ached. I was a non-stop, working, hurting blob. I was visiting doctors, chiropractors, and practicing a small amount of yoga. Keeping up with a heavy work schedule I found no mercy to nurse the pain away. It persisted and grew more intense. Two doctors diagnosed my symptoms as fibromyalgia (they didn't know what else it may be).

Day in, day out, I covered up with smiles and laughter but I didn't find much happiness in life. All the excruciating pain had thrown me into depression.

This is all sounding pretty pathetic, isn't it? Or does it all sound too familiar? I hear every day about the aches and pains of the ones around me. My friends, their friends, their families, and their co-workers are suffering every day with body aches, illness and disease. If I had known how to handle my stress before all of this built up inside me, I would have led a very different life. Things happen for a reason, some say. I believe it was my misery, heartache, and suffering that drove me to these wonderful methods of inner healing. And now I get to share them with you.

Being available to help anyone who is experiencing pain, heartache, stress, or overwhelm is my life's purpose. My mission is to help others the best I can. I'm writing this book for you to move stress out of your body quickly, to induce restful peace of mind, to quiet anxiety and worry, and to lift your spirit to feel incredibly happy!

*Think on those things that bring a smile to your face.*

# CHAPTER ONE

## My Decision

Recently I had to make a very important decision. It was a decision that would cost me approximately $24,000, involving a business I had been building for the past ten years. It was a decision that could possibly change my life radically. One never knows what is around the corner. Will this decision fill me with regret or elation? I was very uncomfortable just thinking of making a change. No, let me take that back. I was excited just thinking about making the change, but deciding to do it put many uncertainties ahead of me. The uncertainties involved relationships I may lose, which was my biggest source of pain. Losing $24,000 a year was my biggest source of worry. I'd reflect on profound phrases like "F.E.A.R. an acronym for False Evidence Appearing Real." "Put your fear under your arm and do it anyway." "Worry is living in a future that hasn't happened."

Days of stomach-grinding had been building. I kept hoping for an obvious sign. I had no one to help me decide what was right or wrong for me. Then, I remembered I do have someone. She's a tender, soft-voiced person, who always sees things clearly, who seldom forces her opinion, who only shares when asked, who doesn't judge. She's always available when I have the time. And yet, I forget to pay a visit when I need her most. I do have someone. She lives very close by, within an arms reach.

But can I trust her? When I pay my friend a visit, can I trust what she tells me?

Yes. My friend has a nickname. She goes by many. Depending on my frame of mind I may call her Gut, Intuition, Center, Inner

Self, Little Voice, God, Divine Guidance, or Higher Intelligence. And if I follow her message, she never, ever fails me.

So why do I doubt this magnificent friend?

Whatever I call it, I am confident that human beings have a center core of wisdom. It is vibrating within at all times. I listen and converse with this center of energy. As I quiet my self chatter and release any held tensions, the wisdom within me talks back.

It is not an auditory voice. It is a subtle feeling. It is a voice in my heart, a strong knowingness. It is always confidant, uplifting and non-judgmental. It is an inner wisdom we call intuition.

*Your center core of wisdom is always at peace.*

## Body Language Takes A New Meaning

*"The cell itself is intelligent. Moreover, its intelligence is contained at a level deeper than its molecules."*
~ Deepak Chopra, M.D, *Perfect Health, The Complete Mind Body Guide.*

I was intrigued to learn every cell in our body is intelligent, as the doctor points out. Science is proving with quantum field theory that every thought we think resonates in our cells. These ideas made me think differently about my body. I asked myself, "If our cells hold intelligence, then should I respect them as such and communicate with them as such?"

I remember one night my back pain was excruciating. It had been culminating over the past three or four days. This night there was no letting up. The throbbing would not quiet. Pillows were stacked under my legs, under my hips, and situated under my neck to keep the piercing pain at bay.

The night wore on. I would sleep five minutes and then I'd awake again to stabbing pain. I remember clearly my forehead was face down; my nose was a bit squished. I was motionless. I'd let my thoughts travel across my back searching for the hub of the pain. I imagined what my pain looked like with fleshy pink muscles and throbbing nerve endings. I tried to imagine how my pain would cry out if it had a voice, and what it would say. I was really engaging my imagination and using my muscles and nerves to talk with each other. I conversed with my back pain as though it were a precious child. "I'm so sorry you're not feeling well. I'm here for you. What can I do for you? I'm listening. I'm here. I'm so sorry I haven't given you attention. What is it you need?"

You see some time ago, I had read a book with a very long title, *Healing Back Pain, The Mind-Body Connection, without Drugs, without Surgery, without Exercise, Back Pain Can Be Stopped Forever.* The author, John E. Sarno, M.D., suggests following the pain with your mind to the center of its source. When you arrive at the core of the pain source, the pain will dissolve. Hold your mind's attention on feeling the center of that pain, and the pain will fade. There will be no pain.

I was in chronic pain with my face buried in a pillow. Dr. Sarno's words kept floating across my mind. I kept my attention on the pain trying to find its center. As I did this the expansive sections of pain started shifting. The outer edges were shrinking in intensity while the pain at its center grew more severe. I kept following the pain with my mind and kept talking to my muscles. I asked them to take me directly to the center of this pain. It required a great deal of concentration but I stayed with it. I asked my back muscles to take me to the center of its pain; I talked to my nerves. I talked to the throbbing sensations. The more I stayed in conversation with my painful self, the more my body responded. The expansive area of pain kept shrinking smaller and smaller. It felt as though everything were alive. The pain was listening to me and responding. Where I had chronic aching across my entire middle and upper back, I now had aching only in the right, upper quadrant. I asked my mind to quiet itself.

"If the mind can reach the source of the pain, the pain will no longer exist," writes Dr. Sarno. I continued seeking the center of my pain. And then, it happened. A section of my muscle which felt like a two inch oval started crunching solely on its own. Yes, crunching like the sound of crispy cereal crunched in your hands. I wasn't touching any part of my back; in fact, I was frozen in place stunned that my muscles were moving on their own. For lack of better words, it felt like the crunchiness melted down my back, dislodging itself and then it dissolved.

My back pain was gone!

My back pain was gone!

My back pain was gone!

The excruciating, chronic pain I had suffered for days was gone! As though someone had come in and massaged me deeply working out the layers of kinks. And yet, no one had touched me. I used my mind to release the painful build up.

I found myself in disbelief that the pain was gone. I kept looking for it to come back. Then I'd say, "Are you crazy? Be thankful it's gone; don't look for it to return."

That was the moment, in the middle of the night, I started believing that the mind can communicate with the body, and the body hears everything the mind has to say.

Trillions of living cells within the human body use a language to speak to us. It speaks in lumps, bumps, tingles, prickles, pangs, aches and pains. Most often we are too busy with the outside world to listen. We ignore it or shrug it off until it screams very loudly to get our attention. Even then do we listen well? In most situations we run to someone else, "What's going on with my body? It's not feeling right." Have you ever listened to your body? Next time something doesn't feel quite right in your body, turn toward your inner energy and ask, "What's going on with you? What are you trying to tell me?"

We haven't been trained to sit quietly with our physical self and tap into our intuition. When I feel a strange lump or bump, tingle or prickly, I sit with my body and ask what's going on with that muscle, or pain, or joint ache. I trust its intelligence will find a way to communicate with me. I am acquiring a new sense of listening.

I am in no way saying not to seek professional medical attention. I am only sharing how for me sitting quietly and talking with my body helps me understand the intensity of the pain /discomfort and the immediate direction I should take to dissolve it.

I am as guilty as anyone with my busy outer life keeping me from focusing and truly listening within.

I do love imagining a future society that has grown sensitive to the body's language. Who knows what healings we could create? Potentially we could heal ourselves before disease takes hold. We could dissolve pain in its early stages through relaxation and focused attention. I see a future where all pain melts away like my back pain did.

The body hears everything the mind is saying.

*Communicate with your body through your thoughts and feelings.*


## Pain Fights to Stay Alive

I've probably set myself up to sound like a loon talking to my body. In two books written by Eckhart Tolle, *The Power of Now* and *A New Earth, Awakening to Your Life's Purpose,* Tolle makes reference to "the pain-body." He describes the pain-body as an energy form made of emotion that lives within us. For the pain-body to stay alive it must be fed. It is primal at survival, feeding or replenishing itself on energy that vibrates at a similar frequency. "The vibrational frequency of the pain-body resonates with that of negative thoughts" which is why only negative thoughts can feed the pain-body. Tolle explains how the pain-body fights to stay alive. It feeds on negative emotions. It feeds on drama. It renews itself. It is a living entity that does not want to be dissolved.

Unattended stress will morph into pain. Be certain not to feed it.

Waves of intention, of feeling, and of stress are affecting the makeup of our physical body.

# No Secure Answer

Back to the very important decision I had to make the other day. My heart knew which decision was best for me yet my head was fearful of making the choice. The doubtful chatter started racing. "How do I replace this chunk of income? What do I do next? Do I start another business? Can I grow my existing business?" Doubt hovered over every question. I had no secure answer.

All the reading I've done for personal growth teaches stepping out, trusting your heart, follow your passion. For days I floundered in the "I don't know" quandary. Then, the light bulb flashed. A shot of awareness woke me up. I realized I was choosing to ignore my true internal response. My inner gut kept telling me the answer; it was my mind that vacillated with an "I don't know" statement.

I acknowledged a response of "I don't know" is an abbreviation for saying, "I'm not ready to make a decision at this time." Or "I'm not ready to dig deep and face my true fears just yet." My deadline was approaching. I had to submit my final answer.

I centered myself with my Higher Consciousness, God, Creator, my connection to Inner Wisdom and, almost instantaneously, a peacefulness and calmness comforted my heart.

As though my heart spoke in words, my inner wisdom said, "Yes. You know what you truly want. Have courage."

I knew my heart was right. I wanted the courage to move forward yet I was afraid of what would lie ahead. I remained frozen with indecision because I did not see any security ahead, nor did I have a plan to follow. Have you heard this one, "What lies at the bottom of the ocean and *twitches*? A *nervous* wreck." There I was: a nervous wreck. I summoned my courage and made my final decision. I resigned from my $24,000 business. I gave up the security.

# Decisions Shrink Fear

Once my decision was made, a wave of peace ran over me, a soft smile came over my face, and a lightness lifted my heart.... "Ahhhhh," now there's the confirmation I was seeking for so many days prior.

The lesson became obvious..... once a decision is made, clarity is your reward.

Resting on my firm decision, new ideas started popping into mind. I learned something really exciting which is when I've accepted something into my heart with no turning back, my brain and thought patterns soon catch up. Miraculously big ideas start to blossom aligning with my heart's decision. Ideas start popping out of nowhere with ways to flourish a new chapter in my life. Exciting avenues to replace my income started formulating. They are not all easy ideas to implement but they are signs of newness and creativity and outlets with a sense of future growth. The excitement makes the fear less significant, In fact, it feels non-existent.

*When you say, "I don't know," what is it you are really saying?*

CHAPTER TWO

# We Are Energy

In high school science class, I learned we are energy. Everything is made of atoms vibrating at very high rates of speed held together by electromagnetic force. The electromagnetic force of energy creates a solid, stable illusion. Atoms are made of electrons, protons, and neutrons, and until recently were believed to be the smallest particles known to man. The science of quantum physics has now confirmed these three particles are made of even smaller particles called leptons and quarks. Leptons and quarks are believed to be the smallest particles in existence at this time.

Atoms exist as constant, high-frequency vibrations. At their deepest center we find only waves of energy and nothing else. The atom emits waves of electrical energy. Energy waves can be measured just as electricity can be measured. There is no material substance to measure within the atom. The space between the atoms is larger than the atoms themselves. The movie "The Matrix" does a splendid job of showing us a visual reality of energy and lots of vibrating atoms dancing crazily all around us.

# We Vibrate into Existence

Our very core is electrical energy. Each of us is vibrating at different frequencies. Perhaps you've experienced this in your daily life. For example, you are in a store shopping. Your mind isn't on anything in particular except the products you're focused on. Someone comes into your close proximity and you naturally move away from that person. Your vibrations are not in harmony. Here is an alternative scenario: another person comes within your close proximity and you feel very comfortable, you may even make a comment or crack a joke. Your vibrating frequencies are similar, allowing a comfort level. Or imagine you are in an enclosed location and someone enters the room. Suddenly the air thickens or perhaps lightens. But you definitely feel a change in the room. As we become more aware of energy vibrations around us, our senses distinguish the higher or lower vibrations. Our awareness also taps into our own vibration and the lightness or darkness it carries.

Dr. Alexander Loyd, N.D, Ph.D and Dr. Ben Johnson, M.D., D.O., N.M.D., have spent years conducting clinical research studies on cellular memories of the body. Our thought energy can become much like a road block in the body and lodge itself in memory cells throughout the body, not just in the memory of the brain cells. There is no part of our physicality that is separate from the rest. So it does make logical sense that the physical body may react or respond to every emotional thought it creates. The more focus or weight we give each thought, the more effect on our body. The more your thoughts create emotion or elation within your mind and heart, a similar energy is created within us. Eastern language refers to this "energy" as qi, chi (Chinese) ki (Japanese) or prana (Indian.) The Chinese have a belief "Chi follows Yi," Yi is the mind's intention or attention.

Good = positive; Bad = negative: our bodies remember and respond to repetitive thoughts.

We attract (draw to us) energy vibrations that match our own. There are so many accepted expressions that allude to this truth, for example, "Water seeks its own level." "Like attracts like." And another by Ralph Waldo Trine: "Faith is an invisible and invincible magnet, and attracts to itself whatever it fervently desires and calmly and persistently expects." However, there is also the adage "Opposites attract." Hmmm, I've got to think on this one relating to an energy field. First thing that comes to mind are polar magnets, because they repel each other.

In October 1966, the country sang along with the Beach Boys.... *"I'm picking up good vibrations, She's giving me the excitations, Good, good good, good vibrations..."* Expressions, like being "in sync or out of sync" validate our instinctive, vibratory feelings, "getting good or bad vibes about a person or a situation" are openly understood. We feel it in our guts. Our thoughts affect our vibrations.

Science has recently developed technological measuring equipment that calculates the electrical and magnetic waves emanating from the heart organ inside a living person. The way it works, the heart radiates energy that reflects intention and feelings into the air space. Whether your intention is positive or negative, this radiating energy can be measured. Research shows that those waves extend many, many kilometers beyond where the heart physically resides. So imagine the energy emanating from the heart of every person is extending into the air space for many kilometers. This is astonishing and it is going on at all times. If science has now proven our electrical waves are constantly emanating beyond our physical bodies affecting the world around us.... wouldn't it stand true those same waves are affecting the world within us as well?

If my thoughts are affecting my body's vibration at all times, then aren't my thoughts affecting the world around me at all times?

*Thoughts become things.*


## Barriers and Shifts

I'm about to share a little more scientific research that validates how our emotions affect the world we live in. We often think we can blow up at a loved one and it will blow over later. But in truth, we are releasing that vibration into the air space. Our vibratory frequency can drag down mankind or it can lift it up to joy and peace.

Dr. David R. Hawkins, M.D., PhD followed the levels of human consciousness charting the electrical system and muscle testing to communicate stress or imbalances in the body. By charting conscious emotions, Dr. Hawkins discovered profound barriers and shifts at different levels of consciousness. He charted these levels and their emotional processes. The research was published in Dr. Hawkins' doctoral dissertation titled *Qualitative and Quantitative Analysis and Calibrations of the Level of Human Consciousness*. Dr. Hawkins believes that every word, every thought and every intention creates what is called a morphogenetic field, or attractor field, and that these energy fields can be measured by a very simple process. This process is a well-established science known as Kinesiology.

Looking over Dr. Hawkins scale one can see a profound shift from destructive and harmful behavior to one of courage and life-promoting lifestyles. It occurs at level 200. Dr. Hawkins uses kinesiology and shows us levels below 200 makes one go weak. Whereas the levels from 200 and higher evoke power, courage, confidence.

"Because the scale of consciousness is logarithmic, each incremental point represents a giant leap in power. As such, one person calibrated at 600 counterbalances the negativity of 10 million people below 200." ~Dr. David Hawkins, MD PHD | Website: <u>Veritaspub.com</u>

In other words, just one person whose life-view emanates bliss, peace, and pure consciousness can counterbalance 10 million people emoting scorn, anger, fear, blame, hate, hopelessness, or shame. That's mind-boggling. Imagine if we could all lift our calibrated emotions to 200 or above. Our planet would be resting in harmony, optimism, forgiveness, understanding, trust and so much more as we move up the scale.

*Every word, every thought, and every intention aids*
*the creation of tissues and organs in the body.*

# SCALE OF CONSCIOUSNESS

|   | Level | Scale (Log of) | Emotion | Process | Life-View |
|---|---|---|---|---|---|
|   | Enlightenment | 700-1,000 | Ineffable | Pure Consciousness | Is |
|   | Peace | 600 | Bliss | Illumination | Perfect |
| **P** | Joy | 540 | Serenity | Transfiguration | Complete |
| **O** | Love | 500 | Reverence | Revelation | Benign |
| **W** | Reason | 400 | Understanding | Abstraction | Meaningful |
| **E** | Acceptance | 350 | Forgiveness | Transcendence | Harmonious |
| **R** | Willingness | 310 | Optimism | Intention | Hopeful |
|   | Neutrality | 250 | Trust | Release | Satisfactory |
|   | Courage | 200 | Affirmation | Empowerment | Feasible |
|   | Pride | 175 | Dignity (Scorn) | Inflation | Demanding |
|   | Anger | 150 | Hate | Aggression | Antagonistic |
| **F** | Desire | 125 | Craving | Enslavement | Disappointing |
| **O** | Fear | 100 | Anxiety | Withdrawal | Frightening |
| **R** | Grief | 75 | Regret | Despondency | Tragic |
| **C** | Apathy | 50 | Despire | Abdication | Hopeless |
| **E** | Guilt | 30 | Blame | Destruction | Condemnation (Evil) |
|   | Shame | 20 | Humiliation | Elimination | Miserable |

*"The numbers on the scale represent logarithmic calibrations (measurable vibratory frequencies on a scale which increases to the tenth power) of the levels of human consciousness and its corresponding level of reality. The numbers themselves are arbitrary; the significance lies in the relationship of one number (or level) to another. Currently, approximately 78% of the world's population is below this significant level. The destructive capacity of this majority drags down all of mankind without the counterbalancing effect of the 22% above 200."*
~ Dr. David Hawkins, MD PHD | Website: Veritaspub.com

*"With each progressive rise in the level of consciousness, the "frequency" or "vibration" of energy increases. Thus, higher consciousness radiates a beneficial and healing effect on the world, verifiable in the human muscle response which stays strong in the presence of love and truth. In contrast, non–true or negative energy fields which "calibrate" below the level of integrity induce a weak muscle response."* ~ Dr. David Hawkins, MD PHD | Website: Veritaspub.com

## Thoughts Create Our Energetic Frequency

When I stumbled upon Dr. Hawkins' Map of Consciousness, I was excited to see validated research. His map charts how thoughts from the mind create different vibrations in the body. Higher vibrations carry more light; lower vibrations carry less light. This correlates perfectly with other findings in current university studies. Multiple research studies are testing monastery monks and their energy frequencies during meditation practices. Their vibratory frequency moves up or down according to their thought patterns. Before I go deeper into the meditation research with the monks I want to share a true story I experienced this morning because it relates to thought patterns and vibratory energy.

I was invited to attend a network business meeting in a town close by. It was my first time there and I faced a group of business peers I had not met before. Everyone was warm and welcoming. The meeting got underway. There were structured formalities of introduction and short presentations flowed around the room. Each person briefly shared their business and highlighted their ideal referral. Every week one member is given ten minutes to highlight his/her business. The idea is to outline for the other members how to find well-matched referral leads for the presenter.

A tall, handsome fellow took center stage. He announced his name and reflected that it was a special day, not only because he was speaking but because it was also his daughter's sixth birthday. I found his comment tender and gave him an invisible high five for bringing his personal life into the presentation. We all felt the warm fuzzies. Mr. Handsome shared his career position as a financial loan officer. Within the next couple sentences he emphasized "so much stress" in his job. I listened with an open mind to learn about his business. I was hearing words out of his mouth like "underwriters are creeps" and he "hates" his processor. Oddly, each time he would use a derogatory comment, the group would laugh. His story continued "I receive no communication; I want to punch him in the face." Everyone laughs. "But he lives across the country and that's the only thing that keeps me from doing it." Everyone laughs. He also said, "... the goal is to hide as much money as you can or you'll pay taxes."

Okay, Okay, I get that he is trying to make us laugh with his sour remarks. And if he had been a comedian I would have gone along with the reality check. Yet, it was his business he was representing and I'm questioning his choice of words.... now granted, I was in the midst of writing this book and working on the chapters about vibrational energy in a room, and in people, etc., and now I am zeroing in on Mr. Handsome's word choice. If every thought and every word carries energy, do I want his energy around me? I wonder. In truth, if I were hiring a financial loan officer, would I want to hire the guy who is "so stressed" and "hates his fellow worker so much he wants to punch him in the face?" I'm thinking not so much. I was feeling repelled. It wasn't resonating. And then I considered that maybe the other friends in the room were just laughing to support the speaker; help him feel better about being up there. Who knows? Maybe they resonated with his stress and hatred too.

Well, this little incident had my mind working hard. I saw on the surface a group that is laughing and making light of things but if we could go deeper, what is truly resting below the surface? When Mr. Handsome gets off work to travel home to his darling six year old, does he leave his stress and hatred at the office? Remember they were his words, not mine.

*Your choice of words reflects your thoughts,*
*attitude, tone, and expectations.*

CHAPTER THREE

# Meditation Changes the Brain

When I was much younger, I would look to the outside world to bring me happiness. My choice of friends, activities, events and food were all indicators of how happy I felt inside. I did not understand that happiness is a choice regardless of the event or food choice. It's exciting to see that science is now using technology to monitor brain triggers to stimulate happiness. Maybe some of us don't choose happy because our brain triggers have no access. Research is proving that mindful meditation brings about a happier way of being. Prayer was not part of the study, but I'm confidant it works in a much similar manner.

Some of the research to which I refer is going on at Harvard and Princeton Universities. Scientists are testing multiple aspects of monks' meditation practices. The research measures gamma wave activity during the monks' meditation. These studies demonstrate meditation's ability to change neuronal patterns, deepen attention skills, and induce tranquility. The practitioner attests to a happier way of being, calmness, and greater harmony with their surroundings and with other beings.

Researcher Jon Kabat-Zinn, Professor of Medicine Emeritus and creator of the Stress Reduction Clinic and the Center for Mindfulness in Medicine, Health Care, and Society at the University of Massachusetts Medical School, concluded **meditation creates permanent changes of the brain.** His tests found considerable more gamma wave activity in the monks tested than in a control group. Kabat-Zinn is one of the first practitioners to record meditation-related health improvements in patients with intractable pain. His stress-reduction techniques are now used in hospitals, clinics and by HMOs.

Richard Davidson is a neuroscientist at the University of Wisconsin's new $10 million W.M. Keck Laboratory for Functional Brain Imaging and Behavior. Davidson ran tests on different aspects of meditation practice. His research concludes: "Their mental practice is having an effect on the brain in the same way golf or tennis practice will enhance performance. It demonstrates that the brain is capable of being trained and physically modified in ways few people can imagine."

Okay, let me list for you what the university studies have validated:

Meditation

(1)  strengthens and changes neuronal pathways,
(2)  deepens attention skills,
(3)  induces tranquility,
(4)  creates a happier way of being,
(5)  creates calmness,
(6)  creates harmony with other beings,
(7)  creates health improvements especially pain related,
(8)  brings about stress reduction,
(9)  enhances performance.


Dr. Edgar Mitchell at the 1997 professional seminar, "Embracing Resonance," presented a model congruent with the theme of our vibrating universe. The model illustrated that *"everything in the universe is energy manifesting itself through unique vibrational patterns. Vibration does indeed lie at the very core of our existence. Its principles are now being deciphered by modern physics, yet they were understood and utilized by the ancients."* ~ Robert T. Hayduk, MA

All of these studies exploring our vibrating, energetic frequencies get me really excited! Using our thoughts to change our vibration can be easily done according to the clinical research. I've started applying these studies to my inner thinking. For example when I'm having a bad day, I stop for a moment and think happier thoughts. I think of a place I'd like to travel and explore. I think of a place I've already been and enjoyed immensely. I think of someone who means a lot to me. I think of the many good things in my life and set the burdens aside for a bit. I think of gratitude. I think of appreciation. I can create anything I want in my thoughts and those thoughts will raise or lower my vibrational frequency. So why choose crummy thoughts?

I shared with you earlier in Chapter Two the measuring equipment that calculates electrical and magnetic waves. It measures waves emanating from the heart that extend into the air space many kilometers; it measures your intention and feeling. Well, here's another bit of cool science in the electromagnetic field of the heart that has been studied in healers. The findings by the Institute of HeartMath indicate that as the heart field becomes more integrated, its capacity to affect biological tissue is increased. Emotions of loving and caring increased with coherence while emotions of anger and frustration decreased. This suggests that electromagnetic frequencies of cardiac energy can be transmitted and received.

Ahh, again, focusing on my heart's intention can change my day. Bring warm, loving intention into my heart space and change my cardiac energy. That's awesome. Can it really be so simple? If I were to focus on my cardiac energy source everyday, could I make awesome improvements in my health? I don't have a long term answer but doing so makes me feel I have more connection to my body's health. It takes that "victim feeling" out of illness.

What a difference we could make on this planet if everyone were to live by these findings. We can use our mind and level of thought to raise or lower our frequency vibration. The first step to calmness is being able to tap into this ongoing vibrating source of energy. When we quiet everything around us for a moment and take pause, we can bring awareness to our inner energy.

The atoms, molecules, cells, tissues, nerve endings, bones, organs, and fluids of our body, each hold a specific rate of vibration. I've been told that inflammation and pain are frequencies vibrating lower than the rest of the body. When I speak to my pain, I ask it to raise its energy vibration to equal the rest of my body.

It doesn't always respond quickly but often it does and the pain level lowers a few notches. When we place our attention upon our vibrating energy we can control our sympathetic nervous system. With a little practice you will achieve calmness, balance, mindfulness and contentment.

I had to use this calming method recently when I fell for a telephone scam. I know, right? Can you believe it? The caller claimed he was from the Technical Department of Microsoft Windows. When I heard him identify himself, a couple thoughts raced through my mind. First: I felt a tinge of guilt for still running the old Windows XP operating system. I knew Windows XP was no longer supported by Microsoft.... so would they be calling me for that? Secondly: The caller knew my full name and had my telephone number. Hmmm, I'm thinking, maybe it really is Microsoft.

So in that light, I entertained the caller by saying, "Yes, this is Deborah D'Aquino."

He went on to say, "Deborah, your computer has been sending multiple error messages into our server which is causing the server to slow down. We cannot operate at full capacity with so many errors coming over the line. May I ask you to go to your computer to check a few things with me? I'd like to get these error messages removed as quickly as possible."

To me it sounded possible. It also sounded a bit fishy but I went along with his request. He asked me to open a viewer by pressing the Microsoft logo and letter R at same time. A box opened.

He said, "Enter this file: E V E N T V W R." I entered the file code. He asked, "Do you see those error messages listed on your screen?"

I said, "Yes."

He said, "That is causing a slow down in our servers. May I help you correct the cause right now?"

I grew more suspicious and said, "How do I know you're from Microsoft?"

His response, "Deborah, I just proved that you have multiple error messages coming from your computer. Didn't I just show you on your computer?"

Again, I said, "Yes."

He said, "Please! We must remove what is causing these errors. We are wasting so much time in this department because of them."

I felt my stress level starting to rise. I also felt massive insecurity because I didn't understand how my computer worked. I'm thinking, "Could this be true? Is he really from Microsoft? He did show me error messages on my computer." I assumed he could see my computer screen. But would Microsoft telephone me with an issue? Well, ..... maybe?

He asked me then to enter this file: "S H O W M Y P C .C O M." He spelled it out, not saying what the word spelled as he moved along. A new page popped up as he asked me to click a box on that page. Now a series of numbers appeared on the page as he asked me to confirm the numbers. I started reading off four of twelve numbers.

Then I stopped and said, "Wait! If you are confirming the numbers then you read them to me."

He said, "No, you read them to me to confirm them."

I said, "If you are confirming them that means they are in front of you. You read them to me."

Then he softened and said, "Oh I'm sorry; I didn't use the right word. I don't have the numbers. Will you please read them to me?"

I can't believe I fell for his good acting. He seemed to be a genuinely nice guy. Part of me did not trust this scenario and yet part of me wanted to trust this person who keeps saying: "I'm only calling to help eliminate this problem with your computer."

It started eating at my gut that I had shared my computer information with a stranger. I became very skeptical and kept hesitating.

He said, "I can see you don't trust me. Let me put my manager on the phone with you." His manager comes on the phone. "Hello this is Alex," the new voice said. "I don't think you understand how urgent this situation has become. Your computer is causing havoc in our servers. If you don't want to correct it now, we will have to block your internet connection."

Now my stress is turning into anxiety. I don't know what decision to make. "Is this for real? Can Microsoft block my internet connection?" Seems like Microsoft is next to God; they probably can block anything they want to block.

I said, "I don't know for sure that you are Microsoft."

Alex got irritated and said, "You don't want to trust me? Fine! Then I will block your computer." And within the next second my desktop went blank. All my icon links disappeared. I tried to stay composed although I became very upset. What had he just done to my computer?

Referring to the blank desktop screen, I pleaded, "Oh please don't do that to me."

Alex said, "Are you going to trust us that we are calling from Windows Dept."

I said, "Yes."

Alex asked, "Are you going to work with us to remove the error problem?"

I said, "Yes."

Alex said, "You are delinquent on your Windows Software Security. We have sent many email requests for you to update your security. You have ignored us."

I replied, "I haven't received any notices from Microsoft Windows."

Alex said, "Is that my problem that you are ignoring our notices?"

I replied, "I haven't received any notices from Microsoft Windows. Please bring my screen back up. Why are you being so mean to me?" I was hoping to tug on his heart strings.

Alex said, "I am not being mean to you. You are not taking this urgent matter seriously! Are you going to work with us to remove the error problem?"

I said, "Yes."

Alex said, "To restore your Windows security there is a nominal fee of $220 for 18 months coverage or $300 for two years coverage."

Once I heard money come into the set up, I grew very suspicious, yet I felt helpless since this guy now has access to my computer. I felt my stress levels rising higher and my stomach is topsy-turvy. I said, "I don't have $200 to spend right now. Please restore my computer screen and give me a number to call you back."

Alex said, "You cannot call us back. If you don't pay the fee, your computer will be blocked until the fee is paid."

I said, "Please, give me a number so I can make arrangements to pay the fee. I will have to make payments. Where do I send it?"

I noticed there were long lag times between his answers to my questions. I sensed they were possibly scanning my computer for passwords or for something that would be bad, very, very bad.

I said, "I'm sorry. I have to call you back." I hung up the phone. I was tweaked and shaky. My nerves were on edge. I had no control over my computer cursor. It kept blinking and moving on its own. It was obvious the scammers were still in my computer.

My stomach was in a state of fearful panic. I also felt incredibly stupid having fallen for a telephone scam. That was something I was confidant would never happen to me.

Along the bottom of my computer screen I noticed the open files and pages they had walked me through...... one by one I closed them and Presto! I could move my cursor again.

I was shaking. I started pacing about the house. I didn't know if these scammers had permanent access to my computer, my mind was racing. Then I caught my image in the mirror. I realized I was letting fear build up within me. I said to myself, "Do what you teach."

I took a few minutes to calm myself. Clarity came to me immediately. It was clear now how to proceed to rectify this situation. I would not let scammers get the better of me. My calming method lessened the fear in me and raised my confidence to clear up the destruction. I made two phone calls to locate my computer genius friend, David. He got a good chuckle over the situation (and my stupidity, I'm sure). Then he advised I shut down my computer. Then, he said to boot it back up and change my administrative password. I followed that by changing all my banking passwords as well. I let go of the situation. I shook it off and announced to myself that that experience is over; it is behind me; I will not be affected by that scam. I let it go.

Life will bring us stressful events day by day. We don't know what is around the corner. We can only choose how to respond *when it happens.* I couldn't say that a couple of years ago. That computer mess up would have stolen my focus for many days.

Today, when I catch myself in a tizzy or I'm feeling too anxious to think straight, I remind myself to take a moment. It only takes a few moments to switch my consciousness into a higher vibration. I stop what I'm doing. I take a deep breath, inhaling slowly. As I exhale, I drop my eyelids. I follow my breathing feeling my body's natural rhythm inhaling and exhaling. I become extremely aware of the air space that is immediately surrounding me. I become aware of the air space within me; I search for the vibrating energy within me. As I connect to it in the present moment I KNOW everything is good. My vibrating energy is perfection. I am good, my life is good, my issues and situations are falling into place. For this moment, I choose to be calm/happy. I assure myself everything is falling into proper place and timing. I will get done whatever lies ahead of me. My unknown answers will be remedied. My projects will be completed on time or even ahead of time. I assure myself with confidence everything is falling into perfect alignment. I align my vibration with all that is good around me.

This takes only a moment. Repeating this process often teaches me to respond to life events rather than to react to life events.

*Take a moment to create internal bliss.*

## Respond or React? That Is the Question

I got out my trusty dictionary to reflect on two words: respond and react. The hard-bound dictionary is still my friend. There is something comforting when I feel the weight of this large book in my hands. I first looked up the word RESPOND. Its description included "something in return," "an answer," "show favorable reaction," and "reply." I then looked up the word REACT. Its description included "exert reciprocal or counteracting force or influence," "stimulus," "act in opposition," "used with against," and "reverse direction."

To me it feels like one word is soft and welcoming while the other is course and defensive. I reread the descriptions. RESPOND includes return, favorable reaction, and reply. REACT includes exert, counteracting force, in opposition, and against. These word choices were taken directly from Merriam Webster's Collegiate Dictionary Tenth Edition.

I have spent the past year or more teaching myself to respond to upsetting situations rather than react to them. It is especially challenging when a partner wants to disagree or defend their point of view and they are "reacting" all over me! I want to react as well, but it takes discipline to remain calm, to think straight, and then I can respond.

According to the studies outlined in the previous pages, I charted some of the most common emotional feelings into two clear columns. One column produces Health, the other column produces Sickness. Reactions to life situations more than often fall into the Sickness column. Responding to life situations usually requires more thought and tends to fall in the Health column. Do you run your day responding or reacting?

| RESPOND VS REACT W/ EMOTIONAL FEELINGS | |
| --- | --- |
| RESPONDING<br>requires Thought,<br>Produces HEALTH | REACTING<br>requires No Thought,<br>Produces SICKNESS |
| Love | Anger |
| Joy | Fear |
| Happiness | Hatred |
| Gratitude | Jealousy |
| Appreciation | Envy |
| Thankfulness | Resentment |
| Sharing | Hoarding |
| Acceptance | Rejection |
| Peace | Shame |

These are just a few of the emotional feelings that resonate as vibrations within our physical body. Words listed under the Health column tested to vibrate higher than the words listed on the sickness side. Can it be possible that in our near future we will manage our health through mental mind/body approaches?

It seems it is possible according to Herbert Benson, an associate professor of medicine at the Harvard Medical School and president of the Mind/Body Medical Institute at Beth Israel Deaconess Medical Center in Boston who studies advanced forms of meditation. He says, "My hope is that self-care will stand equal with medical drugs, surgery, and other therapies that are now used to alleviate mental and physical suffering. Along with nutrition and exercise, mind/body approaches can be part of self-care practices that could save millions of dollars annually in medical costs."

In the early 1980s, I was managing a shoe store in Laguna Niguel, California. My maturity level was not very high. I was young and very much into my image and ego. I was quick to react to a situation instead of responding. My daily routine dealt with numbers, personalities, hiring/firing, time schedules, inventory, balance sheets, customer complaints, and all the many hats of managing a brick and mortar store. I was single and had a crush on the store manager next door. He had shown interest in me as well. We had been on multiple dates and our relationship was blossoming.

I had a dependable sales staff. There was my assistant, Jim, and two darling sales girls, Stacey and Annmarie. I recall having one more employee on staff but his name escapes me right now. Stacey and Annmarie were young, vivacious, pretty girls that, I admit, stirred a little jealousy in me. My dating interest, Geoff, wasn't bashful about charming the girls and flirting when he could get away with it.

As a manager, I took on a lot of responsibility. I didn't realize how much I liked to be in control but looking back, it's obvious. One evening I left my assistant in charge so I could have the night off. The following morning I arrived early for work and I found a small serving cart in the center of my office. It was noticeably out of place; it had been put there sometime during the night. At the center of the cart was a blob of transparent whitish goop. My mind started racing. I immediately drew conclusions and suspicions. I didn't know who was involved but I was livid that this was left for me to find. I didn't want to think any sex was actually going on in my office but I feared my new love interest was involved. Oh, I hoped not. Most managers in the mall arrived much earlier than the staff. I walked directly next door and, with a demanding voice, asked Geoff, "Were you in my office last night?" I was reacting to my own conclusions. Did I respond by taking a quiet moment for deep breathing, finding my center, and then thinking through the situation first? Heck no, I confronted Geoff with an accusatory demeanor. I prejudged that he was way out of line having fun in my store and in my back office. I was spitting out my disgust and disappointment, giving him no time to speak. The thought that he might have engaged in sex with my employee pricked at my underlying jealousy. My jealousy made me lash out. How could he be flirting with my sales staff when he was suppose to be attracted to me?! How could he?!

Geoff had never seen me so irate. He was becoming irritated quickly. He finally got a word in and said, "We thought you'd think it was funny. We left it there because we thought it was funny and wanted you to see it." He then explained what had happened. It was after hours, the store staff was putting away shoes in the back room when Geoff popped his head around the corner and started being goofy to get some laughs. When they had finished up with the store chores, Stacey washed up. As she squeezed hand cream from a tube, it flew about four feet and landed in the center of the work cart, making everyone laugh. One of them suggested leaving the cart for me to see and on it goes. For what they experienced as a silly, fun, end of the day episode full of laughter, I found as a biting, jealous, hurtful expression because I reacted from a low energy place inside me.

I continued to feel hurt and angry many hours into the day. I spilled anger all over Geoff, leaving a grey cloud on his day. As my staff arrived, I lashed out with anger and disappointment towards each of them, adding an ugly energy into their day, too. For hours, thoughts continued to roll over in my mind causing energy in me that was far from love. Anger and jealous vibrations continued to pour out of me long into the day. I kept thinking about it over and over in my mind, trying to justify why I was right to be angry. I replayed the whole episode from my point of view. I searched for justification continuing to feed the angry energy. It grew larger and larger.

If we could see a person's energy encircling them in a color, there must have been a sour grey color emanating from me all day and spewing onto the customers as they entered my store. I'm sure I greeted them with a lousy attitude as well, because, let's face it, I was not having a good day. All that unnecessary, ugly energy was permeating the air space, floating into the mall, resting on people's shoulders, commingling with their vibrations as well. I wonder how long it takes for negative energy (that's floating around in the air) to dissipate?

My bad energy affected everyone that day and probably for a couple days to follow. All my staff kept conversations to a minimum and Geoff avoided me for a few days. It was no fun. How often do we let similar sour energy infiltrate our cellular being and move into the air space? Or how often do we walk into a mass of sour energy from someone else without knowing it? Is it easy to just brush it off? Or does their energy penetrate our skin and color our own mood? Who's to know, who's to say? To think all of that ugliness may have been avoided had I taken the time to respond appropriately and not react as I did.

*Our thoughts create energy vibrations that expand into the air space around us.*

CHAPTER FOUR

Misery Loves Company

Over the years I've attended numerous transformational semi-
nars and workshops. I hear the same message at each: what I
keep replaying in my mind, what I keep mulling over, rethinking,
and contemplating is what will keep showing up in my life epi-
sodes. Negatives will show up and positives will show up. When
I change what's playing in my mind, the new change will show
up in my outer world as well. Changing my internal environment
changes my external environment.

Newtonian physics from the seventeenth century based its
theory on belief that there is only matter and nothing else – the
whole universe is a machine, made of matter, and so are we. Slowly
science is putting to rest the antiquated beliefs and medicines that
arrived through such misjudgment.

Much of medical science today is still based on Newtonian
physics. That is certain to change in the upcoming years as we
understand energy and our effect on it. Energy exists although
we can't see it. So goes the same with our vibratory emotions. We
cannot see love, but we can feel it. We can't see disappointment,
but we can feel it. We can't see envy or jealousy, but we can feel
them. We can't see joy in one's heart, yet as one jumps up and
down and expresses their joy, we can feel their joy in us, too. We
can be stirred to feel someone's sorrow just by reading a note or
hearing a song. It is our thoughts that move us to feel those emotions. Our thoughts soar through our energy meridians instantaneously. Kinesiology is proving successfully with muscle test-

ing that thought exists everywhere in the body. Many forms of energy healing like EFT (Tapping), Acupressure, Acupuncture, Reiki, Theta, Emotion Code, Healing Code, and Chakra healings are proving to heal successfully at a percentage rate higher than symptomatic relief through medicinal prescription treatments. Energy healing methods are becoming more welcomed as alternative choices for pain. It is a beautiful blending of ancient practices with today's scientific discoveries.

Thought energy travels throughout our body, up and down meridians. Negative energy from an emotional event may become stuck causing a kink or blockage in our energy pathways. The negative energy lodges in our cellular memory. These kinks or blockages invite chaos into our cellular system.

Dr. Alexander Loyd, N.D, Ph.D and Dr. Ben Johnson, M.D., D.O., N.M.D., have spent years conducting clinical research studies with cellular memories of the body. Dr. Loyd is a number one best-selling author and has been featured on NBC, ABC, CBS, FOX and PBS News programs as an expert in identifying and healing the source issues underlying illness and disease. Their findings I shared with you in Chapter Two, but I will repeat it here since it is directly relevant. Our thought energy can become like a road block in the body and lodge itself in memory cells throughout the body, not just in the brain. There is no part of our physicality that is separate from the rest. So it does make logical sense that the physical body may react or respond to every emotional thought it creates.

Lots of chaos in our cellular structure breeds stress in the system. Stress leads to:

| | |
|---|---|
| Discomfort | Inflammation |
| Unhealthy Bacteria | Irritation |
| Free Radicals | Bad Moods |
| Disease-like Symptoms | Bad Attitudes |
| Cancer Cells | Disgruntlement |
| Headaches | Unhappiness |
| Body Aches | Misery |

The old adage applies. "Misery loves company." "Like attracts like."

*It is a continual circle: Negative thought leads to Blockage leads to Chaos leads to Stress leads to Negative thought to Blockage and on and on it goes.*

# Mind Secrets

A lkaline is a big buzz word right now. The Health and Wellness industry is emphasizing the importance of keeping the internal organs healthy by eating alkaline foods like cruciferous vegetables, leafy greens, green tea, fruits, and lemon water. That seems easy enough for keeping the body healthy. As for keeping the mind healthy, I have learned there is also a simple secret: thinking higher thoughts of thankfulness, appreciation, gratitude, compassion, sincerity, acceptance, kindness, joy, happiness, and truthfulness. It's also why expressions like "I love you" feel so good to say and feel so good to hear.

I may sound like Pollyanna, looking for the good in everything. But what's the negative to that, really? I feel so good when someone tells me qualities they like in me. I may voice a humble disagreement, but, nonetheless, it does make me feel really good. As a result I find I like that person a whole lot more for saying such nice things. Whereas, when someone points out my faults or shortcomings, whether true or not, it doesn't stir good feelings in me. I feel rather deflated. Their point of view doesn't help me feel good. As a result I find myself not liking them as much as I did before. Am I alone on this one? Or is this pretty general as we humans go?

Attitude affects everything. Cleaning up your attitude, removing the criticism, looking for what is good in each situation, lifts the energy of the room and the relationship. I work at keeping my attitude uplifted every day. Granted I'm still a work in progress but I am consciously aware all the time, so much so that I catch myself when I'm not thinking uplifting thoughts about a person. Oops.

Many years ago, Oprah Winfrey interviewed Dr. Maya Angelou. Dr. Angelou inspired and changed my perspective with a very simple statement. She was speaking about children and the sensitive understanding children possess. She shared that a child instinctively knows as he enters a room how much he is loved by the glimmer in your eye. He also knows if that glimmer is missing. Angelou's profound statement excited me. The light came on. A glimmer in your eye can be seen by everyone - not just children. I decided right then to work more diligently on showing my eye glimmer to everyone. Let them know I care about them. It's true everyone has a glimmer they choose to turn on or off. Why do we ever let it turn off? Why not show that glimmer when you open the door to receive someone you're expecting? Why not show that glimmer when students arrive at your class? Why not show that glimmer when your spouse enters the house after being away for a few hours? Why not show that glimmer when you answer the telephone? It's not so hard to let love pour through you for no reason. It lifts the energy of the room, the energy in the welcomed friend, and the energy in you.

After my Angelou revelation, I started studying the glimmer in people. People with glimmer will light up a room. Children possess a strong glimmer until it gets taken away from them. You can see it in their eyes. You can hear it in their voice. George Harrison sings it well, "They wear their thoughts on their faces." Keep an eye open. Watch and listen for the glimmer in folks. More often than not, it seems to be missing.

A girlfriend of mine is a very caring person. Before telephones had caller I.D., every time I telephoned her she would answer with a very rough, "Hello!" If I had to paint her face as she's greeting me, I would paint a furrowed brow and tightness in her jaw. It comes across as though I am interrupting a very busy, important person who has no time for this call, or any call. Once I have shared who it is calling her, her entire demeanor softens, there's a lightness and excitement in her voice; it's almost as though a different personality has come on the line to greet me. If we could have a do-over, it would feel so welcoming to hear that glimmer in her eye even answering the phone.

"It's easier to change him than to change me!" To change what's going on inside of us boils down to changing what we thought was right. Our perspective is the best perspective – that is why we would follow it, right? To open our heart and change our glimmer, change our thinking, change our attitude, change our life! That's huge!

## We See It As We Think It

My brother, Billy, is a great guy. He colors his world in optimism. He is always willing to help out others. When he is asked, "How's it going?" Billy's reply is always, "Awesome!" Life events unfold for Billy with an easy flow. Even when the flow is interrupted and others may see a challenge ahead for him, Billy always keeps a positive demeanor. His attitude is "We'll do alright." Soon enough, awesome life situations do indeed pop up for him. I have another friend who is the exact opposite of Billy. This friend I will not name. This friend thinks people suck and most of her engagements become entanglements she views as "sucky." People are out to get her or rip her off. Everything is a challenge. Her daily activities and situations tend to match her perception. Unfortunate situations somehow find her, one unfortunate event after another.

Our personal life experiences create our perception of the outside world. No two perceptions are alike.

As we change our perception, little by little we bring calmness into our living space. We become more harmonious in our daily grind. We offer more kindness to strangers. We experience more kindness from strangers. We acquire a new awareness that everything around us is temporary and less important. The energy we send out is the vibration that will mirror itself and reflect back into our life. Mindful meditation slowly changes our neuronal pathways to soften our perception of the outside world. Calm and happy is a better choice towards softening our perception of our chaotic world.

Mahatma Ghandi did a terrific job of creating a difference by keeping a calm attitude and nonviolent approach. Philo Gabriel, Yahoo contributor, shares much about Gandhi's philosophy in an article, "The Philosophy of Gandhi: Concepts of Truth and Nonviolence." He reflects on Gandhi's attitude as "Respect for our fellow rational beings necessitates treating them not only as potential recipients of truth but as potential sources of it. We do this by listening to them and by exposing ourselves to their beliefs and values. For if we care about truth, we will welcome discovering it in others, even where this requires adjusting or relinquishing our own position. Psychologically, we often find it more comfortable to rationalize retaining our present beliefs and attitudes, whatever their merits, but like so many other temptations, this is something that must be resisted if we are to live up to our potential as truth-seekers."

Ghandi is saying to open our minds, for every being may be a source of potential truth. We should treat them that way. Listen to them. So often when in conversation, I find myself excited or eager to share my own ideas and opinions. As a result, I'm not truly listening; I'm waiting to jump in to talk. Ghandi says "For if we care about truth, we will welcome discovering it in others, even where this requires adjusting or relinquishing our own position." Discovering in others and adjusting or relinquishing our own position – what a great selection of words and depth of meaning.

How often do I relinquish my belief to consider a new truth? That is asking me for deep vulnerability.

I find myself most joyful when I'm producing, sharing and interacting with people. I find myself most stressed when I'm not getting things accomplished and I feel my opinions are not being heard.

I have fallen into the techy world of social media, emailing, keeping up, and sharing opinions and quips. Much of it is just about being heard. I feel I've accomplished something when sharing my opinion. I do enjoy sharing information and thoughts with my friends. Even brief communication helps me feel I've given some attention to those I care about. It is a crazy, new, wonderful world we have created in social media but it can be exhausting. For it, too, can become a stress producer. Is the busyness of our lives helping us feel productive and somewhat more accomplished? Keeping all things in perspective, what purpose is it serving in my life picture?

## Practice Makes Close To Perfect

Someone once told me, "Prayer is talking with God. Meditation is listening to God." I liked that; it rang true in my heart.

When I am praying, I feel I am interacting and conversing one on one with God.

When I'm meditating, I feel fully connected to omnipresence. A presence that is so much greater than I am and yet I am part of it. There is abundant wisdom. There is knowingness without words attached. I suck up the feeling like a sponge but often I cannot put words to those feelings. The feelings are far greater than any words can convey.

I attended my first yoga class when I was 19. The soft lighting, faint music, and simple stretches were soothing to me. My instructor guided me to turn inward and feel what my muscles were doing as I held a pose. I was taught to breathe differently, to push my stomach out as far as it will extend while inhaling, to continue breathing as air fills my abdomen and lifts into my lungs and chest. As my chest rises I become aware of my expanded lungs pressing against my back and I feel my breath moving into my neck muscles. We're asked to hold the breath and then exhale slowly letting the breath release and all the muscles relax, and again, asked to hold with no breath for a few counts. Simple breathing had suddenly become challenging work. How was it that I had been living for 19 years and could not recall ever paying attention to my own breathing apparatus? It was all very different and foreign to explore these inward feelings.

The instructor ended each class with an exercise called *savasana*. We would lie on our backs, legs comfortably apart, toes to the ceiling, arms extended away from the body, palms up. Using guided thought we would relax each body part: starting at the feet, working up the legs, hips, torso, hands, arms, shoulders, neck, and each section of the face, ears, and forehead. By the end of the ritual, my body was completely relaxed. I was fully conscious but I could no longer feel or sense any part of my body. I imagine this is what pure consciousness may feel like if there is no body to contain it: a vast openness with no judgments or attachments. It was the closest thing to perfect peace I had ever experienced. Ahhhh! I loved that feeling.

Awareness of my own being-ness started to unfold. Hatha yoga presented a new exploration of my body, my breathing, and the power of my mind. My mind worked with my body asking my muscles to stretch to their maximum and then relax. Asking my mind to relax was another challenge.

My first achievements with meditation were also my first experiences of an inner awareness. This new awareness let me experience a profound connection with the ever-present and eternal mind I call God, in a new personal way. I was raised catholic and had spent many hours in prayer. This new experience resonated differently than prayer did. It required a great deal of concentration but the effort was worth the reward.

After 42 years of practice, I have gotten much better at this. I practice daily meditation and I can pat myself on the back for good achievement. I've advanced to being able to meditate anytime, anywhere. I can access a peaceful wisdom within and let go of any chaotic stress. A number of friends converse with me about meditation. I hear from them that they don't get anything from it and confess they are "not doing it right." I remember those days well when I misunderstood meditation. I assumed there was a right and wrong way to do it. I imagined if I were meditating correctly my mind would have no thoughts. I assumed I would see my third eye and travel into wondrous spaces. I think I imagined meditating would feel like being on a drug of sorts. I didn't quite know what to think since I had no point of reference. I would sit in meditation position and asked my thoughts to go away. I waited, hoping my thoughts would scatter. I waited for colors to fill my mind's eye. I waited and waited and waited myself into frustration. My expectations were so far beyond the baby steps of practice; I led myself right into disappointment. You know how it goes when one gets disappointed. Well, for me anyway, I have a tendency to avoid things that bring disappointment. So meditation for me was a slow learning process.

I'd love to share everything I've learned with you. In fact, in this book, I am going to give you an easy five minute meditation that works wonders. I want to let you in on something big. Something no one told me when I was first learning. I had to arrive at this on my own through many years of practice and frustration. All of my spiritual teachers explained, "Thoughts will come up but do not dwell on them." What I did not get from my teachers was what to do when those thoughts do pop up. When I'm told not to attach to a thought that's the first thing I want to do. Well, here's the thing. As thoughts come up turn your attention away from the thought, instead focus on what you are feeling inside, focus on the quiet space inside your body and your thoughts will fade away into the background. There are chaotic thoughts and sounds going on at all times, let them all pass by without grasping or contemplating. Focus on the peace that is also around you at all times. This is meditation.

*"Let expectations fall away."*

# CHAPTER FIVE

# Changing My Internal Environment Changes My External Environment

The first four chapters of this book have addressed the effects of thought on the body and the recent research to back up these statements. We addressed how thought exists in the form of energy, how energy can be measured, and how energy can become lodged in the body much like a traffic jam on the roadway. The jammed energy is called emotional blockage. Emotional blocks can be shifted and released by raising your frequency vibration. Vibrational frequencies lift when the intention of your heart aligns with your choice of thoughts that measure high on the Scale of Consciousness (see Chapter Two.) High ranking thoughts include love, truth, courage, neutrality, willingness, acceptance, reason, joy, peace, gratitude and thankfulness. These are not levels of intellect; they are levels of the heart's compassion.

These next few chapters will focus on raising consciousness willfully and lifting our energy vibration. It will be very easy for you to learn and practice. The more you practice the faster you will become at releasing stress.

I am going to introduce five simple steps of awareness. I selected these particular five steps from a successful program I have been teaching called Green Tea Meditation Transformation. The program stirs inner awareness regarding health, love, desire and forgiveness. Through weekly classes, participants experience a shift in their daily routine. Students have shared remarkable uplifting changes in their business life, their personal relationships and their own perspectives after practicing once a week over eight to ten weeks.

Five minutes a day of similar consciousness uplifting will positively change your internal environment thus changing your external environment.

If you like this five-step abridged version, you will truly love the complete Green Tea Meditation Transformation.

The five steps of conscious awareness to remove stress are:

- Awareness of Being
- Awareness of Thinking.
- Awareness of Physical Body
- Awareness of Unlimited Love
- Awareness of Forgiveness

I will devote a chapter to each step for clarity from start to finish.

As you explore these techniques you may be thinking, "This is too easy! How can this help me?" You're right, it is easy. It is simple. Most of life's answers are simple and easy. It is human ego that makes everything difficult and hard to manage. It is so easy to bring peace of mind into our situations.

---

To find more information about Green Tea Meditation visit **www.debbiedaquino.com.**
Receive FREE give-a-ways and discount offers from Debbie D'Aquino, and be first to receive new material and event announcements. Enter your contact information at **www.CalmistheNewHappy.com.**

---

CHAPTER SIX

# Awareness of Being

Doing, doing, doing: it's the way of life these days. Everyone is so busy doing stuff. Even when it feels like we're not doing anything we're usually doing something. I'm probably doing something mindless: watching TV or Youtube or following Facebook. I like working Sudoku puzzles while the television runs a mindless show. I am totally entertained while I feel like I'm doing nothing, yet all my senses are engaged; I am far from doing nothing. My mind and brain are not resting, in fact, they are working. You've heard the expression "working hard or hardly working, which one is it?" I am relaxing my body but my mind and brain are fully engaged; my neurons are triggering.

Taking time during your day to focus on doing nothing re-energizes your body physically, emotionally, and spiritually. Most of us are challenged to stop all the busyness of the day, all the "doing." The mind swirls with what ifs and should haves and gotta dos and showing up and getting here and getting there. "I have so much on my mind today. I don't know how I'm going to handle everything on my plate right now. My bank account needs attention. I worry about my family, my house, my upcoming deadlines, my performance, my physical health, my food choices, my decisions, my abilities, my strength or lack of all of it. I am already worried that I'm not getting done the things I really need to do. How can I possibly stop to do nothing?"

Our western culture is so far removed from quiet time within. To stop all doing sounds like impossibility. To pause in your day almost requires a "How to" manual. Okay then, here is the first lesson in your "How to" manual. STOP!

Find an inviting area to sit and stop everything on your mind. Let everything rest just for this moment. Let everything around you freeze in stillness. You can afford a moment of time for yourself.

Straighten your spine. Close your eyes. Practice BEING present. Release everything around you. Release everything on your mind. Any thought beyond this exact moment is considered doing.

Focus on being. You are a living being. Focus on your core center of energy.

Become aware of your breathing. Inhale and exhale. Keep your spine straight. Stay focused on your breathing; focus on how it feels to breathe. Become aware of what your body is doing as you inhale and exhale. Continue breathing slowly. Keep your spine straight. Feel your shoulders relax. Feel your neck relax. Your arms, your chin, your jaw, and your facial features relax. Every part of your body is relaxing. The tension is leaving your head. Tingles of relief replace the tension.

With eyes closed, become aware of the air space around you. Become aware of the air touching your skin and touching your clothing. It is extremely close to you. Become aware of the air space within you. Accept the air space around you and the air space within you as one. There is no boundary. Feel your center core of energy. Feel the flow of energy coursing through your body. Energy flows through your arms and legs and torso. Become aware of your energy vibrating within. Stay with this awareness. Accept the peace that breathing brings you. Accept the peace that awareness of being brings you.

It only took a minute to bring about an Awareness of Being: Be present, Be mindful, Be relaxed.

# CHAPTER SEVEN

# Awareness of Thinking

It is a wondrous thing how we can think without choosing to do so. We think through every waking moment and even through most of our restful sleep. It requires a conscious effort to stop the thinking process. The more we practice resting our thoughts, the better we become.

Most of us have no idea how to stop our overworked brain from thinking. I use the following visual in my class to give my students a new perspective about the flow of their thoughts.

Imagine a faucet in a bathtub has been running full stream. As one turns the knob to close the valve, the water flow slows to a mere trickle. The trickle continues to thin out until it is just a series of water drops streaming from the faucet head. The drops follow one by one quickly. You hear drip, drip, drip in quick succession. As time passes the forming drops start to slow to drip... drip... drip. You hear the dripping sequence slow even more with a quiet space between each drop. By its sound you can envision the drops slowly taking form as they stretch from the faucet head and hit the bottom drain. The sound gap is growing greater and greater. Drip...... Drip...... Drip...... Eventually the drops from the faucet are fewer than the long stretch of silent time between them. Imagine even more space between each drop of water falling. Concentrate on the open space of silence between each droplet. It's the quiet, open space. Now imagine the drops are your thoughts. There is a small stretch of time between each thought popping up. Reach for the small stretch of time: the open, quiet space between each thought. The open space is a space of nothingness, of peace of mind. The more you practice, the greater the quiet, open space will grow.

Let's practice letting go of thought for a brief moment. Let your "to do list" relax. Let your chores and appointments rest for a moment. Let your thoughts of the outside world drift by you. Focus on the dripping faucet. You may say to yourself, "Drip, drip, drip, drip," in very fast succession. Then slow down the pace to let your self wait between each drip. Slowing the pace will let the word drip become a soothing mantra. Your body will relax between drips. Let no other thought come between the words, drip.

As your mind slows down from its frantic pace, release and let go of your thoughts. Ask your thoughts to fall into Divine Order.

Divine Order houses a magnificent filing cabinet. Imagine this filing system is the most elite, organizational tool ever invented. It is far greater than any human design. It stores your thoughts in perfect order and delivers your thoughts back to you the moment you need them. They are held in Divine Order for retrieval at your will. You no longer have to keep so much on your mind. Everything will be held in perfect order when you are ready to address it again. Imagine an automated filing cabinet designed for your access only. This fabulous cabinet keeps all things in perfect order. The instant you release a thought it immediately becomes filed.

Freeing the mind of thought for small moments of time helps balance the physical, emotional, and spiritual energies within us. Practice stringing a couple seconds into many seconds without thought. Even to accomplish a few seconds without thought is excellent.

This process will add energy and clarity to your day.

# CHAPTER EIGHT

## Awareness of Physical Body

Day in, day out, the physical body works as a well-programmed machine. Did you know the mind can not distinguish reality from imagination? What we say often enough is what we program in our subconscious mind. What we program is what we attract into our life. I practice every day, sending my subconscious new programming information. Changing the chatter in my head from sounding like Negative Nellie to talking to a friend I love very much. I look myself in the mirror and say, "I love you," to myself. I look into my eyes and say, "You're terrific." I work at it every day because I am not in a high, positive state of mind naturally, although recently my new interior chatter is growing closer to my brother Billy's awesome-tude.

You *can* create a calming interior for yourself with a little practice every day.

This is a simple "go to" that I practice everyday. Find a relaxing position. Ask your body to let go of all its tension. Relax your neck and shoulders. Bring your awareness to focus only on your here-and-now sensations. Concentrate solely on your facial features. Is your forehead furled? Lift it to feel smooth for a second, and then let it relax. Is your mouth turned down? Raise each corner into a lifted smile, and then let it relax but not turn down. Are your eyebrows pinched? Lift your eyebrows upward stretching the pinched skin then let them relax but not pinch. Are your jaw and neck tense? Move them gently to release any creeks or pops and let them relax. Go inside your body with your mind. Become aware of what is going on inside your body. Acknowledge each organ functioning at its peak performance. Your lungs are expanding and contracting. Your heart is overflowing and refilling with perfect rhythm. Your kidneys are cleaning your blood. Your bones, muscles and tendons absorb nutrients keeping you healthy. You are a working masterpiece. You are glorious and you don't even know it. Let gratitude well up from your center. Send appreciation and gratitude into every magnificent working part doing its job inside of you.

Focus on gratitude and appreciation: not in thought but through emotion, not with intellect but visceral. Send those feelings into every cell, nerve, tissue, and fiber of your body. Send gratitude into every limb, joint, muscle, bone, tooth, and nail. Send appreciation into your blood stream.

You are glowing with compassion from the inside out.

# CHAPTER NINE

# Awareness of Unlimited Love

If it were possible to collect all the love you have ever known, how much could you gather? Imagine collecting all the love you have ever known. Gather all the love you have ever received, all the love you have ever been given, all the love you have ever given away. That would be quite a collection. Now if you could collect it in your large, brawny, invisible arms how would that feel? How would it feel to have so much love you can barely contain it all? And yet it is all yours.

I am going to walk you through an expanding exercise. Love continues to pass through us with no end. When we experience this we also raise our vibrational frequency to a much higher level. The higher our frequency vibrates the more resilient we become to negative energies. So let's gather up as much love as we can imagine!

Relax into a comfortable position. Let go of any tension across your face, neck, shoulders and throughout your body. Find a quiet place in your mind. Now imagine it's possible to gather all the love you have ever been given. In an instant gather all the love you have ever felt, gather all the love you have ever received. Gather all the love you have ever given away. Imagine you are able to basket all of this love into your invisible arms. Imagine gathering this love in your invisible arms and even catching the overflow. It's a huge amount of love. With your imagination compress this over-flowing love into a small ball between your invisible hands. Compress the ball even smaller down to the size of an avocado seed, then down to a peach seed, and compress it even smaller to the size of a lemon seed. This seed contains unbounded, radiant, pure, sacred love.

With your imagination, place this sacred seed of love in the center of your heart. Feel the wonder of holding this eternal love within you. Give it permission to grow inside your heart. Watch it slowly expand in size like the rays of the sun reaching out and increasing in size. It grows to the size of a dime, and to the size of a quarter and to the size of a golf ball. It is expanding to fill your entire heart space. Like the rays of the sun reaching outward your sacred love is filing your entire chest cavity reaching into every cell of your torso, your shoulders, arms, hips, thighs, knees, calves, ankles, feet and out your little toes. Your seed of love expands into your neck, jaw, cheeks, forehead, ears, scalp and every follicle of hair. Every living cell of your body is absorbing pure love.

Imagine this love is expanding beyond your body. Watch it reach into the air space around you. Everything with which it comes into contact, it penetrates with love. You are radiating pure love.

Stay with this unending source of love expanding from your heart and penetrating everything around it. Continue to expand your love further. Watch its rays touch and penetrate everything it reaches. It travels through your neighborhood, touching every person in its path. Penetrating love finds every friend and family member, every stranger and acquaintance, every pet and animal filling each with unbounded love. Keep sending out love watching it expand across town, expand across your state, your nation, the oceans, continents, and sky.

Your love is boundless. Let it expand even further stretching around the planet and into the heavens. Your love is stretching throughout our galaxy and past multiple galaxies. Your love is expanding to the outer edges of the Universe and beyond the limits of the Universe.

Like the rays of the sun, for this moment, you are pure Love expanded beyond the limits of the universe.

Hold this feeling of expanded Love. For this moment, nothing else exists.

Feel the presence of this fully expanded Love beaming from your heart.

Focus on the grandness your Love is radiating.

Now welcome ALL that Love back into your heart space. Welcome it in. Receive it with open hands and open heart. You have been fully expanded far into the outer edges of the Universe. It will take a little time to collect all that Love back into your heart.

Welcome all this Love back into your heart. This fully expanded love fills your consciousness with wisdom and goodness. Everything is coming into you with perfect order. Love carries calmness and joy. Love carries peace and acceptance. Love carries confidence.

Welcome this Love back into your heart with a trustful knowingness that your projects will be completed in perfect time, your relationships will heal as you permit them, and your to-do list will be easily accomplished. Trust that bills will be covered even though the money path is not clear right now. Know that Love will not leave you to suffer. Everything will be done in divine order in its perfect time.

Acknowledge you are full of Energy. Acknowledge you are full of Joy.

CHAPTER TEN

# Awarness of Forgiveness

It wasn't until recent years that I learned to appreciate how much I am a participant in the circle of life. While I used to think I was an observer in my life, I have grown to realize I am the designer of my life. My thought choices, reactions, and responses are creating its quality. I am the participating artist of my beautiful life unfolding.

This artist messes up a lot. I have found myself reacting quicker than my better sense would have it. I am then left disgusted with my own actions and word choices that I used without compassion. I will mentally beat myself up. I get an aching in my stomach and I replay the scenario over and over until that's all I'm thinking about. Well, now I've learned a new remedy I absolutely love. It removes the icky feeling of guilt or regret I'm holding inside. It brings me quick clarity and intuition for what to do next. It is called, Ho'oponopono.

Ho'oponopono, an ancient Hawaiian method of problem solving, is my favorite source of healing. It is based on belief that existence is a gift from Divine Intelligence; it creates a process of repentance, forgiveness, and transmutation. This special Hawaiian word, Ho'oponopono, means "to make right" and it is applied to make right things in our lives that have disturbed or upset us. Its concept is so bizarrely simple it is hard to believe it could work. But somehow it does. I have used it upon many small, trivial situations and I've used it on mighty disagreements. It is amazing how things correct themselves.

The most memorable time I've applied Ho'oponopono was after a disagreement with someone I care for deeply. We were on the phone and a comment came up one time too many. It hurt my feelings the first time it was mentioned which was many, many years ago. It had come up a few times since then and I continued to brush it under the rug. Now it comes up again and it triggered such a hurt I could no longer keep my mouth shut. It felt like she had poked at me one time too many and my feelings got ruffled. Instead of letting it brew any longer I spoke up and said, "That really hurt my feelings." I think I expected and anticipated a humbling apology. To my surprise instead I got a defensive response from her which inflamed my hurt ego even more. Then I got wimpy and defensive trying to explain why it hurt me. Before we ever got close to apologies she hung up on me! Now I was really ruffled. For a fleeting ten minutes I felt like I would never speak to her again, not ever in my life! I'm done.

After the burning hurt started to simmer, the replay of our phone conversation continued in my head. What I said, what she said, what I said, and back to what she said. It made my stomach ache and I could not shut off the player in my mind.

I felt guilty. I felt small. I felt silly. I felt right! I felt defensive. I felt disrespected. I felt unloved.

I let this mass of unsettled feelings swirl inside me for half a day. I was constantly aware of my unsettled spirit and then I said, "No more!" I walked myself to my favorite meditation chair. I got comfortable and starting repeating the Ho'oponopono phrases: I love you. I am sorry. Please forgive me. Thank you. I said them not to my friend, but to the Divine.

I said them over and over and over and over. Many times I repeated these phrases until I felt a clearing in my heart. I felt a forgiveness sweep over me and a light joy come back into my spirit. I felt a resurgence of love for my dear friend. I knew the disagreement was over.

The importance of the disagreement was so much smaller than the importance of our love. I let a few days pass, and then

I called her. She was happy to hear from me. Nothing was ever mentioned about my hurt feelings or about her hanging up on me. I was totally okay with it. The air was cleared. My perspective had changed through Ho'oponopono.

It works incredibly fast. It works in traffic. It works on broken electronic situations. I have had so many small changes in my life by applying the Ho'oponopono. It has even changed my life philosophy evolving human participation in this fabulous creation around us.

Another true Ho'oponopono story resolved a money problem. My dear friend, Geri, was battling a number of financial challenges all at once. She shared her quandary with me just as friends do. While I didn't have an immediate material resolution, I did ask if I could share something spiritual with her. She's so funny, as she quipped, *"Heck yeah, it can't hurt."*

I asked that she repeat these four sentences throughout her day. Every time she thought of her perplexity, repeat these four sentences. I asked her not to go too deep trying to understand how this could work but to just try it. Quite honestly, I didn't have all the answers to the questions anyway. I spoke the four sentences with meaning behind each word. *"I love you. I am sorry. Please forgive me. Thank you."*

We went over them a time or two to get them memorized. Then Geri decided to write them on paper. I reminded her that she was not saying this to anyone in particular. I noticed that this part really threw her off so I said, "If there has to be somebody you're speaking to then direct the phrases to yourself. Think of your situation and say them over and over."

A week later, Geri came to me and said, "Deb, I've got to talk to you." A tone in her voice had me thinking the talk was not going to be a good one. I was so wrong. She said, "That Ho'oooey hooey ha thing — it really works! I kept saying it just like you told me. Stuff started happening for me. I found someone to rent the extra room in my house, so that is bringing in another $1200 a month. And then I met a darling cosmetologist who is available to rent a station in my salon. Now that will bring in another four hundred a month. I can't believe it's all coming together for me. It's working!"

Okay, so it may all be coincidental but the coincidence came with perfect timing, yes?

I shared the sentences with another friend, Mary. Mary had hoped to heal her relationship with her brother. They had not spoken for two years. And there was a lot of animosity built up between them. I shared that it is not important that the person be present. Just think about him and your part in the relationship and say the four sentences, over and over.

Mary loves to run five miles every morning. She started the very next day on her run. She climbed to a pinnacle point and while looking out over the ocean, she repeated her sentences: "I love you. I am sorry. Please forgive me. Thank you." Again and again, many times over, she repeated the words. Then she continued her run. Mary kept up with this program every day. Approximately two weeks passed and she excitedly told me her brother called out of the blue. They talked for the first time with no strain to the conversation. My friend exclaimed: "I'm so happy! It works!"

I found this special healing from a book called *Zero Limits, The Secret Hawaiian System for Wealth, Health, Peace and More* written by Dr. Joe Vitale and Dr. Ihaleakalá Hew Len. In fact, I have read it three times and refer back to it often. It was not an easy concept for me to accept. It is unlike anything I have ever heard about or explored. The authors teach the use of these four phrases and by golly gee stuff happens. Things correct themselves or get better. Try it for yourself, without judgment. Repeat the four phrases in any order you choose. Continue to repeat the phrases until you feel an energy shift inside. Sometimes I say, "I love you" twenty times in a row, then I move onto "I am sorry," twenty times in a row. "Please, forgive me" ten times in a row. "Thank You" one hundred times in a row. Whatever feels right for you, in any order. Just say it!

I've heard that I love you and I am sorry are the two hardest things for mankind to say.

You can never truly forgive someone until you forgive yourself.

Meister Eckhart said, "If the only prayer ever said was *Thank You*, it would be enough."

*"I love you. I am sorry. Please forgive me. Thank you."*

# CHAPTER ELEVEN

# Calm and Happy in Five Minutes

Once you have read and practiced chapters six through ten, the 5-minute list will be easy to implement. Simply remember the five steps of conscious awareness to remove stress and you will reach calm, within yourself, in just five minutes.

The best way to learn and experience the process is to read through the first minute, and then give it a try! Explore the sensations being suggested. Read through the second minute and then try it. Explore the sensations. Read through each minute separately and test yourself. Each minute is a small meditation itself. Focus on the feeling of the message putting less importance on the words or thoughts in the message and more importance on the feeling. Do this while letting your heavily-thinking brain relax.

Thought travels instantaneously. The instant you think it, the deed takes place. Practice this over and over.

Suggestion: Record the step by step instructions, then listen to the play back to experience the calming effect.

**STEP BY STEP INSTRUCTIONS:**

1$^{ST}$ Minute: STOP ALL DOINGNESS. (Awareness of Being)
- Straighten spine.
- Close eyes.
- Breathe in deeply. Exhale while relaxing your shoulders, neck, and arms.
- Continue breathing and relaxing, keep spine straight.
- Become aware of the Air Space around you.

- Direct your awareness inward.
- Become aware of the Air Space within your body.
- Become aware of the Energy Source in your body.

2nd Minute: LET ALL THOUGHTS FALL INTO DIVINE ORDER. (Awareness of Thinking)
- Imagine putting all your thoughts into a filing cabinet off to the side.
- Close the drawers.
- Know your thoughts are in perfect order.
- They will be there when you need them.
- Let all thoughts fall into Divine Order.
- Thoughts will resurface only when you need them.
- Focus solely on your breathing.

3rd Minute: FOCUS INWARD. (Awareness of Physical Body)
- Become aware of your physical body, organs, bones, and infrastructure.
- Send Gratitude into your cells, tissues, nerve endings, tendons, blood stream.
- Send Gratitude into every cell of your body, filling every limb, joint, and hair follicle.
- Feel Compassion for every physical part of your body.

4th Minute: EXPAND LOVE. (Awareness of Unlimited Love)
- Imagine collecting every bit of Love you have ever known, all the Love you have ever received, all the Love you have ever been given, all the Love you have ever given away.
- Collect all this Love by gathering it into your invisible arms.
- Gather this Love into your arms. Now compress it into a small ball between your invisible hands, and compress it even smaller into the size of a seed.
- This is a seed of pure, energetic, vibrating Love.
- Place this seed of Love into your heart space.
- Give this seed of Love permission to grow inside your body filling every cell, nerve, tissue, and fiber.
- Watch rays of Love expand into every physical part of your body.

- Watch rays of Love expand beyond your body reaching into the air space around you.
- Keep watching rays of Love expand beyond you, filling the room, penetrating everything in your neighborhood and across town.
- Let your Love expand even further covering your state, country, oceans, and sky.
- Expand your Love even further stretching around the planet, into the heavens.
- Expand your Love even further beyond our galaxy and past multiple galaxies.
- Send your Love as far as the mind can conceive to the outer edges of the Universe and beyond the limits of the Universe.
- Feel the presence of Love beaming and radiating from your heart.
- Hold onto this wondrous expanded feeling of Love.
- Welcome ALL that LOVE back into your heart space.
- Welcome it in.
- Receive it with open hands and open heart.
- Know All Love pouring into you is Good and Pure.
- Everything is coming into you with perfect order.
- Love carries a security that your projects will be completed in perfect time, your relationships will heal as you permit them, your to-do list will be done. Bills will be covered even if the money path is not clear right now.
- Know Love will not leave you to suffer.
- Everything will be done in divine order in its perfect time.
- Acknowledge you are full of Energy.
- Acknowledge you are full of Joy.

5th Minute:  HO'OPONOPONO  (Awareness of Forgiveness)
- The way to best forgive another is to first forgive yourself.
- Turn your focus inward.
- Repeat these four phrases to yourself as many times as it feels right:
    I Love You

I Am Sorry
Please Forgive Me
Thank You
- Feel the Peace within.

Before you open your eyes, tap into the feeling within you. A deep feeling of thankfulness should be resonating inside you right now. Capture that feeling and surround it with Joyfulness. Take this feeling into your day. Let everyone you meet see the Joyfulness within you. Take this feeling into your week. Let it touch every person you encounter.

You have successfully raised your vibratory scale of consciousness much higher. You are resting at the frequency of Love, Joy, or Peace (somewhere between 500 and 600) It feels fantastic. Hold a mindset of accomplishment, appreciation and gratitude.

Re-examine your expectations. You will get better results each time you practice Five Minutes to Calm and Happy. Stay focused on your breathing and your body sensations. Communicate with these sensory experiences acknowledging their presence.

Become aware of the here-and-now experience. Stay in this present moment not the moment that is coming up or in the moment that has passed. Stay focused on what you're feeling instead of your thoughts.

*Create Love, Peace, and Joy in every part of your body.*
*Just think it up!*

---

If you have been enjoying "Calm is the New Happy, How to Get There in 5 Minutes" visit **www.debbiedaquino.com** for more programs with Debbie. Receive FREE give-a-ways and discount offers and be first to receive new material and event announcements. Enter your contact information at **www.CalmistheNewHappy.com**

---

# CHAPTER TWELVE

# When There Isn't Five Minutes

In the midst of a busy life, sitting quietly for five minutes isn't always possible. For those times when you don't have even five minutes, try some of my power tools to change your mood or perspective. Remember we cannot change anyone but ourselves.

Perhaps you are in a slow-moving check out lane, or a traffic jam. Your workload just increased with no extra hours to get it done. You're feeling anxious about a presentation or performance. What ever the situation, it is causing your stress level to rise; overwhelming frustration is starting to rise up.

Stress is simply fear. It may be fear of what is to come. It may be fear you won't meet a deadline, or arrive on time, or perform, or deliver. Stress is the thought pattern you hold concerning the deadline, or traffic, or extra workload. The greater it builds it becomes overwhelming frustration and anxiety.

Power tool processes reflect qualities of intelligence, talent, and strength that make quick effective response possible. Use one of these power tools to bring you back to center and clarity. These tools bring us into the present moment instead of anticipating the upcoming minutes or hours ahead. Being in the present moment of NOW is always comforting.

## Power Tools

Choose one of the following and practice when you're feeling stressed while waiting in line or stuck in traffic or slowly losing your patience with the kids.

**Breathe Deeply**

Deep breathing can be enjoyed anytime, anywhere. This effective tool releases negative emotions and anxiety. Deep inhales and exhales carry oxygen into your cells for optimal performance. Deep breathing lowers stress levels. Purposeful deep breathing throughout the day will increase energy and lift brain fog. Awareness of breath brings us into the present moment.

**Quiet the Mind**

Give your brain a job by telling it to settle down. Stop thinking. Ask it to feel calm for a few seconds. Your mind will respond and start to feel calm. Ask your body to relax for a few seconds. Your body will relax.

**Become Aware of Surroundings**

In the present moment, become aware of the air space around you. There is air brushing against your skin. Become aware that you are enjoying free air to breathe. Between you and the next material object is a quietness of air space. Become aware of that space. Enjoy its perfection. Become aware that all of your body parts are working at this moment, without your supervision. Become aware of the countless amount of colors within your eye view right now. You are part of the surrounding scenery in this beautiful chapter of life.

**Smile for No Reason**

Daily challenges, traffic, unexpected upsets are life's way of strengthening us. Negative life moments can break you under pressure. To counter this, smile for no reason. For example, in your car, put a smile on your face for no reason. Make a game of it. You'll find some people smile back. When another driver makes a stupid move, smile! You don't necessarily need to smile at the other driver, although that's cool too. Simply smile for your own self-preservation instead of building into a state of driver's rage. If something really messes up at home, stand there and smile. A real smile makes it exceedingly hard to get angry. Our brains are not wired to smile when we are irritated. It throws things into another basket. When I catch myself reacting instead of responding I tell my face to smile. I remind myself not to dwell, the entire incident is gone, it's in the past, and it's not worth ruining my day. Face the irritation and Smile. Most of all have fun with it. Try smiling for no reason.

### Show Gratitude & Appreciation
Nothing will make your heart lift more quickly than sharing gratitude and appreciation. It becomes more fun giving it away than receiving it. Just like smiling when not expected, if a friend messes up and is expecting you to become irritated try this instead: show gratitude and appreciation, leaving them dumbfounded. It takes the edge away. They are not sure how to respond. They become grateful themselves. Welcome the task at hand with gratitude and appreciation. Your life will soar with reciprocity. Your happiness meter will shoot to the top!

### Use Your Childhood Imagination
Let your mind have its own vacation. Imagine silly, crazy, wonderful things. Let go of any rigidness or impossibilities. When you're waiting in a checkout line, imagine something fun like flowers growing out the ears of everyone ahead of you. Imagine building a birdfeeder that flies around to the birds instead of the birds having to fly to it. Imagine a mountain of green one hundred dollar bills piled high when you open your front door. Imagine your own crazy, wonderful thoughts and always think of things that put a smile on your face. Imagine how happy you are right now.

# No Silver Bullet

To wrap it up, I'd like to say there is no one silver bullet that works for everybody. Thought is instantaneous. Just think it and then focus on how that thought feels inside you. Thinking happy thoughts is most healing. Let's play the Happy Game. Just think happy with me for a moment. "I am so happy right now. Everything in my life is working for me. Everything I want comes to me without fuss. Everything around me is exactly as I want it. Everyone I love is happy with me. Life is wonderful. I'm so happy."

If those few thoughts helped you feel good even for a moment, try thinking similar thoughts more often. Why keep the crummy thoughts going?

There is no one silver bullet for everything. I have an assortment of applications I use for stress and pain relief. I have been able to share a slice of what works well for me. My pain story from the introduction of this book is much longer and more complicated than what I wrote on these pages. I did not want to lose focus of the book's purpose by writing too much about healing my health. I'm very pleased to share that just about all of my body pain has left me. It's been a long journey of exploration, study and application. I've found a lot of success through Mind-Body connection methods, meditation, prayer, EFT, paleo eating, Kangen® water, and daily exercise. I no longer struggle with fibromyalgia, herniated discs, sciatica, arthritis, or migraines. I continue to keep myself Calm and Happy with prayer and meditation every day.

For You, I wish an abundance of peace, love, light, goodness, and prosperity.

May you live in Health, Wealth, and Joy, always!

I invite your sincere conversations or questions.
Please contact me through my Website:
www.debbiedaquino.com and www.CalmistheNewHappy.com

---

Thank You for staying with me to the end of the book!
I want to stay in touch with you, too.
Receive FREE give-a-ways and discount offers from
Debbie D'Aquino and be first to receive new material
and event announcements. Enter your contact
information at **www.CalmistheNewHappy.com**

# RESOURCES

I send gratitude and appreciation to all resources used for inspiration, education, science, and history.

(Chapter One)
Braden, Gregg. *Secret Ancient Knowledge: Gregg Braden – The Divine Matrix*. YouTube <youtube.com/watch?v=MRedvbARVhM> Gregg Braden revisited: Full conference "The Divine Matrix". January 21, 2013
Chopra, Deepak. *Perfect Health, The Complete Mind Body Guide, Revised Edition*. New York. Three Rivers Press. 2000
Sarno, John E. *Healing Back Pain, The Mind-Body Connection*. New York. Warner Books. 1991

(Chapter Two)
Anando. *The New Science: We are made of Energy, not Matter*, Osho News Magazine, Science and Nature, Dec. 10, 2011
Loyd, Alexander, PhD, ND, and Ben Johnson, MD, DO, NMD *The Healing Code: 6 Minutes to Heal the Source of Your Health, Success, or Relationship Issue*, Grand Central Life & Style. February 9th 2011
*Scale of Consciousness*. veritaspub.com
Thompson, Carla M. *The Map of Consciousness-Hawkins' Scale*, January 19, 2012, Copyright 2012
http://happy-firewalker.blogspot.com/2009/06/dr-david-hawkins-map-of-consciousness.html

(Chapter Three)

Cromie, William J. *Meditation changes temperatures: Mind controls body in extreme experiments.* Harvard Gazette Archives

Danzico, Matt. *Brains of Buddhist monks scanned in meditation study.* BBC News. New York. Sunday, April 24, 2011

Hayduk, Robert T. *Sound and Resonance.* Hemi-Sync®, MA Journal. Fall 1997

Kaufman, Marc. *Meditation Gives Brain a Charge, Study Finds.* The Washington Post. Monday, January 3, 2005; Page A05

May, Meredith. *Stanford studies monks' meditation, compassion.* SFGate. Sunday, July 8, 2012

Vitale, Joe, and Ihaleakalá Hew Len. *Zero Limits, The Secret Hawaiian System for Wealth, Health, Peace, and More.* Hoboken, N.J., John Wiley & Sons, Inc. 2007

http://voices.yahoo.com/the-philosophy-gandhi-concepts-truth-nonviolence. Philo Gabriel. January 13, 2011

http://news.harvard.edu/gazette/2002/04.18/09-tummo.html

http://www.washingtonpost.com/wp-dyn/articles/A43006-2005Jan2.html

http://www.newscientist.com/article/dn4116-brain-study-links-negative-emotions-and-lowered-immunity.html#.VO5m-WyzFo4k  (*Proceedings of the National Academy of Sciences, DOI: 10.1073/pnas.1534743100*)


(Chapter Eight)

Vitale, Joe, and Ihaleakalá Hew Len. *Zero Limits, The Secret Hawaiian System for Wealth, Health, Peace, and More.* Hoboken, N.J., John Wiley & Sons, Inc. 2007

# THANK YOU

Thank you for joining me on this journey. Life brings its stressful challenges. When it does, I hope you will choose to respond rather than react. I hope the same for myself, too.

I'd love to hear from you any time at CalmistheNewHappy. com. Also, please let me know if you hold any interest in joining me for an online webinar on similar messages of this book.

1. Subscribe to CalmistheNewHappy.com for free to keep up on my latest writings and offerings.
2. Suggest this book to friends and everyone who might enjoy it.
3. Share this book on facebook and google plus.
4. Stumble or tweet it.
5. Review the book on your blog.

# ABOUT THE AUTHOR

Debbie D'Aquino is a transformational coach inspiring people to reach high levels of health, wealth, and joy. She stays very involved in her local community as a dance instructor, a meditation leader, and a wellness counselor for Enagic Corp. She lives in a charming little town along the Pacific Ocean near Los Angeles, California, called San Pedro.

Debbie was born in Pennsylvania. At age twelve, she moved with her family to Hagerstown, Maryland, where she attended high school and community college. Shortly after earning her Associate's Degree in Business Administration, she left the east coast to travel the country. Debbie settled in Laguna Beach, California. She pursued her interest learning more about inner bliss by completing a Teaching Certification in Yoga Asanas, a Certification in Touch for Health Training, and a six-month study program in therapeutic massage.

At the same time, Debbie worked as a textile artist in Laguna Beach from 1974-1983 and gained recognition as a talented fashion designer. An intense desire to design professionally led her to study at FIDM Los Angeles where she was awarded her Design Certification in Fashion in 1984. She then launched what became a successful 20+year career designing sexy lingerie for corporate America, followed by an activewear collection under her own label.

Debbie is enjoying the newest chapter of her life as a transformational coach focused on creating a better you, inside and out. She loves teaching, sharing, guiding, and motivating. She is changing lives everyday and would love to share with you, too. You may contact her easily through the website www.debbie daquino.com and www.CalmistheNewHappy.com.

# ~ ATTITUDE ~

The 92-year-old, petite, well-poised and proud lady, who is fully dressed each morning by eight o'clock, with her hair fashionably coifed and makeup perfectly applied, even though she is legally blind, moved to a nursing home today.

Her husband of 70 years recently passed away, making the move necessary.

After many hours of waiting patiently in the lobby of the nursing home, she smiled sweetly when told her room was ready.

As she maneuvered her walker to the elevator, the attendant provided a visual description of her tiny room, including the eyelet sheets that had been hung on her window.

"I love it," she stated with the enthusiasm of an eight-year-old having just been presented with a new puppy.

"Mrs. Jones, you haven't seen the room.... just wait."

"That doesn't have anything to do with it," she replied. "Happiness is something you decide on ahead of time. Whether I like my room or not doesn't depend on how the furniture is arranged... It's how I arrange my mind. I already decided to love it."

~ www.mountainwings.com

Made in the USA
Middletown, DE
13 August 2018